THE SETTING
OF THE SUN

MARY MCAVOY

This is a work of fiction. All of the
characters, names, incidents,
organizations, and dialogue in this novel
are either the products of the author's
imagination or are used fictitiously.

Library of Congress Cataloging-in-Publication Data

McAvoy, Mary.
  The Setting of the Sun: a novel/Mary McAvoy

ISBN 978-0-6156-0461-9

2012951553

With love
to my mother

Mary Louisa O'Hearn Armitage
(1922 — 2011)
who was a native of
Lawrence, Massachusetts
and who edited
The Setting of the Sun
the year before she died.

I am happy she saw that this book
is dedicated to her, since it did
not publish until after her death.

Though she moved from Lawrence in
the 1940s, her love for the city
stayed with her always.

In memory of
my grandmother
Louisa Nancy Breen O'Hearn
and
my in-law grandmother
Mary "May" Cantillon McAvoy,
who were born in 1898 and who
spent much of their lives
in the city of Lawrence.

Prologue

It was early June. The day was
warm and dry. Anne had opened the
windows throughout the house. The songs
of the springtime birds drifted on soft
breezes through each sunny room.

But the melody of the birds was not
what Anne was hearing. In her mind she
was involved in a conversation she and
her husband Tom had had the night
before. They had talked about their
twentieth anniversary, which was in just a
few weeks. They had decided that they
could not afford to buy each other gifts.
With the boys' college tuitions, and the
parochial school expenses of their four
other children - little Maggie included this
year for the first time – there was no extra
money.

It was Tuesday, the day Anne
changed the bed linens. She tightly tucked
the corner of a top sheet, after

meticulously folding the cotton to make it secure. This was the fifth and final bed that needed her attention. With the two older boys away at school, she found that this weekly chore was completed in less time, allowing her a more leisurely pace and more time to think.

Anne sat on the edge of the bed - the bed Tom and she had slept in every night since they'd married - thinking that she still wanted to give Tom a gift. She thought of all Tom meant to her. Theirs was a rare love. Her very essence was wrapped up in the love between them. If anything happened to Tom, if he died, she could not imagine living. She felt that he was so much a part of her, that her existence, for her to be, depended on him.

Anne began to contemplate the verb "to be" – the tiny verb that defines the enormous meaning of our being. After a little time, Anne's mind started to gather words and phrases, and to arrange them in rhythms and rhymes. She realized that she was piecing together the start of a poem, and that this would be her gift to Tom.

There were times in Anne's life when her thoughts and emotions were so entwined that writing a poem was the only way she could unravel the intricacies and express herself. Rambling prose could not convey the intensity of her thoughts and feelings.

She hurried to her desk and took out a pencil and her poetry notebook. She quickly opened to a blank page and scribbled across the top of it "The Setting of the Sun" - and before it could leave her mind, Anne wrote the opening line of a poem that would stay in her heart until the day she died –

"To be, for me, is to be with you at the setting of the sun..."

I

Early Morning

Anne opened her eyes to a new day. Her eyes scanned her bedroom. Maggie came through the door just in time to answer Anne's two immediate questions.

"Why is my blue dress hanging on the closet door? Where are we going?"

Maggie paused at the end of her mother's bed.

"Mama, remember? Today's Pa's funeral." Maggie reached and put up the window shade letting in the morning light.

Anne had a vague sense about Maggie's answer, though not a fully comprehending one.

Waking had become a bewildering event for the old woman. Her morning awareness did not necessarily connect to the day before. Each day was now an isolated piece of time.

Before opening her eyes to this day, she'd lay still, in dreamy consciousness, delighting in the scent of coffee. She'd remembered that Maggie was at her home, so it must be Maggie who had made the coffee. But she couldn't explain Maggie's presence. Then, as if on cue, her daughter had knocked softly on her bedroom door.

"Are you awake, Mama?" Maggie had whispered as she entered the room. And seeing her mother, not much more than a wrinkle in the blankets, her heart went tender. It was then that her mother had asked why her blue dress was hanging on the closet door, and Maggie had felt her heart break a little more while helping Anne remember that this was the day when she would part forever from her one true love, Maggie's father Tom.

Now, as Anne's eyes adjusted to the light coming through the open shade, the phone rang and Maggie hurried from the room.

"Give me a minute to get this call, Mama. Take your time getting up. It's just seven."

As she left the room, Maggie called over her shoulder, "We won't leave till quarter of ten. I'll be back to help you shower and dress."

Anne sat up slowly. Leaning her back against the headboard, she paused and gazed around the room she'd awakened in for seventy-five years. She did not focus on distinct things - like the double row of framed photographs of her children when they were infants, or the wooden crucifix that held a dried palm frond against the wall. Nothing in particular on her bureau caught her attention. All that her eyes saw was a palette of familiarity.

But the presence of her blue dress hanging on the outside of the closet door continued to convey meaning to her. It told her that this day would bring something different than her usual routine.

After a minute, she pushed the sheet and blanket from her legs and paused again. Easing her legs over the edge of the bed, she sat and rested, just as she'd been taught by a visiting nurse. At the moment, she couldn't recall why she did this - but it was a habit she repeated each day.

She slid her feet into her waiting slippers and said to no one, "I'll just sit another minute."

She looked at the large knuckles and pattern of veins on the hands resting in her lap and didn't recognize them as her own. In time, her right hand trembling, she reached for her cane. With her left hand, she pushed herself from the bed and stood. Again she paused, waiting until she felt steady, and then she began her walk to the bathroom.

This path was the only one she still tread with some confidence. Leaning gently on her cane, she slowly made her way, using her other hand to keep her balance by holding onto her bureau and then by pressing the side of her hand against the stretch of wall that had a strip of wainscoting.

Once in the bathroom, moving as if in a world without gravity, her frail arms and hands slowly and deliberately brushed her teeth. Then she arranged her things for her shower. She put her towel and face cloth over the edge of the tub, and draped her underwear, slip, and stockings on the towel rack.

When Maggie returned, she helped her mother into her shower chair. While she shampooed Anne's thinning white hair, in her mind Maggie saw the faded photo of her mother, the one that always made her mother laugh and comment, "I was called 'the raven-haired beauty'!"

Maggie gently washed her mother's fragile skin. As she did so, she saw not just her own future, but the past - as she tenderly bathed the arms that had cradled her as a baby, the breasts that had nursed her, and the once strong back of a woman who had weathered more heartbreak than should burden one person. The legs that powered her mother as she swam in the lake of long-ago summers, gliding effortlessly with one or two children clinging to her with glee, now had the look of malnourishment. Age had claimed her. Maggie saw in her mother her own approaching fate.

Maggie towel dried her mother's hair.

"Tell me again where we are going."

"To Pa's funeral, Mama."

Maggie's patience with the endless repetition of questions from her mother was grounded in love. She treated every moment with her as a gift and an occasion to give back the love that had been given by Anne to her and to so many others.

As her daughter helped her put on her clothes, finishing with the blue dress, Anne watched in the mirror. Through the frayed fringes of her old mind, her thoughts slipped into a moment lost in time, a moment scattered and dispersed, though her memory could reassemble it as if it were still real.

She saw herself as she was at age fifteen - hopping up and down, the fabric of her blue dress ballooning and swaying in the breeze. She held both hands with her best friend Annie, who likewise jumped up and down as the two girls laughed with unrestrained delight. Oblivious to everything but their joy, they were making their way home along the streets that led to their houses. Though they were not yet halfway there, the twenty-minute walk had already lasted twice that long as, with each step, they paused and reviewed every minute of their afternoon spent with the two boys who had captured their young hearts.

Anne smiled. "I loved your father from the day I first met him..."

Maggie added, "...on a Sunday afternoon, at the church spring picnic."

The story was one Maggie knew by heart – not just the story of that afternoon, but the family history that led to it. Her mother and her mother's best friend Annie, had grown up in houses side-by-side in Lawrence, Massachusetts, a mill city on the Merrimack River, not far from where the river poured into the Atlantic Ocean.

It was 1913 when the two girls had spent that Sunday afternoon with their future husbands. Each girl was third-generation American, of Irish descent - their ancestors having arrived in the first wave of immigrants who came to Lawrence in the 1840s.

Lawrence was a planned city. Each commercial building, each street, and all the housing had been carefully thought out. But the city planners could not have foreseen the flood of immigrants who would crowd into Lawrence and there was simply not enough housing.

Anne and Annie's grandparents and great-grandparents had endured the growing pains of Lawrence. Anne had told her children stories about those early days. They heard of the shantytowns scattered within and outside the street grid of Lawrence, where houses were primitive structures - cold, damp and drafty with dirt or packed sawdust floors.

Living in these conditions, Anne and Annie's earliest American relatives had survived the epidemics that claimed many lives. They rode out the turmoil of politics and the violence that came with the ethnic strife and bigotry that plagued Lawrence for the first decades of its existence.

Anne wanted her children to know that their ancestors had proven their value in the hierarchy of labor, rising in importance as each new wave of foreigners (the Canadians, the Germans and the English) arrived in the city through the remainder of the 1800s.

The turn-of-the-century world in which the girls were raised was far different than the harsh lives of their earlier relatives. The life into which each of these girls had been born was wealthier and healthier, and included fair hope that life could be happy.

Born in the second-to-last year of the nineteenth century, these girls enjoyed homes that were filled with beautiful furniture and drapes, fine mirrors, oriental rugs, polished sterling accessories and fine bone china place-settings. New immigrant women, hired by their mothers to help them get their start, assisted with the care of their homes and the preparation of meals.

Along the stretch of Haverhill Street where the girls lived, and within the walls of their homes, they experienced a life that they knew was more privileged than the lives of many other children in the city. They saw this daily in their classrooms in grammar school, where all nationalities and economic classes were represented. Here the bigotry against Catholics that plagued Lawrence for generations played out often as Anne and Annie walked home from school and heard the taunts, sometimes successful, to lure the Catholic Irish boys into a fight.

Now, nearly a century later, Anne sat at the breakfast table, lost in thought.

She turned to Maggie.

"Do you remember Annie?"

Maggie knew that the question was literal though somewhere in her mother's mind was the knowledge that Annie had died years before Maggie was born.

Still Maggie answered, "Yes, I do."

It was not a lie, as Maggie had heard about Annie all her life and she felt as if she had known her.

After several quiet moments, she heard her mother muse, "I hope she'll be there today."

And here Maggie found herself in that frequent dilemma that had to be worked out in seconds. Should she play along with her mother's confusion or correct it? The former was easier, but done repeatedly it banished her mother to a world not connected to reality, where Anne still had the ability to reside.

So, Maggie said in a matter-of-fact tone, "Mama, Annie died long ago. She won't be there today."

Her mother stared at her, looking through her to the past, trying to recall the truth, while trusting that Maggie would not lie to her.

"Hmmm," was all she said. She finished her breakfast silently.

Though she sat in silence, her mind was actively revisiting a string of memories of her friend. She loved to think of the first moment she was aware of Annie. It was their first day of first grade. Annie sat at a desk to her right, quietly sobbing. Noticing that the top button of Annie's dress was unbuttoned at the nape of her neck, and assuming, in her five-year-old mind, that this was why the girl was crying, Anne whispered to her, "Your button is unbuttoned. I'll fix it."

Anne had expected that this would soothe the girl, and that Annie would stop crying. Instead, Annie lowered her head to her desk and howled out loud. Anne's eyes went wide as she sat paralyzed by what she had caused. But the well-trained teacher came to Annie's aid, and achieved what Anne had not been able to – to assure Annie that her baby dolls would be fine until she returned home at the end of the school day and finished the story she had been telling them before she had left for school.

As the teacher attended to Annie, she spoke kindly to both girls.

"I need help with something. You each have the name Anne. How will you know to which one I am speaking when I call on one of you?"

The girls looked blankly at the teacher and then at each other. Helping them along, the teacher asked, "What are your middle names?"

Simultaneously, the girls blurted out, "Elizabeth," and then looked in astonishment at each other.

Their teacher smiled.

"Well, that's a lovely coincidence, but it doesn't help us. What are you called at home?"

Annie's eyes were now drying.

"My brothers call me 'Annie!'"

At this point in the story, Anne always thought of the envy she felt in that moment - Annie had brothers, while she had not one brother or sister. Their teacher then asked Annie if it would be alright if she were called Annie at school.

"Oh, yes!"

So, from then on, she was Annie.

And from then on, for all intents and purposes, Anne had a sister.

Annie's golden-brown eyes were large and lively. Her face was oval and she had straight auburn hair that behaved, however she wore it. In the sunlight it looked more red than brown. Anne wished her own black hair, with its weather-sensitive curl, had just a bit of Annie's care-free attributes. Annie envied Anne's statuesque height and posture, and her natural athletic strength and agility. The girls' ivory-tone cheeks easily flushed. Anne's blue eyes could be both softly feminine and strong-willed. Her personality was kind and honest, but always forthright.

When the girls were in third grade and soon after her father had a promotion at work, Annie's family moved into the house next door to Anne's on a section of Haverhill Street that housed the families of men who had management positions in the mills. Anne's father was paymaster at a mill, overseeing the disbursement of weekly wages. Annie's father worked for the Essex Company, the city's founding company, as an engineer who monitored the daily fluctuations in the river's water flow as it passed through canals near the mills.

Lovely Victorian homes stretched along this area of Haverhill Street. Trees lined the sidewalk and nearly every house had a wrought-iron fence with a gate that opened to a walk leading to double front doors. The large homes were similar, although each family's decorative taste gave the homes a distinctive look. The houses sat close together, all with a small patch of lawn in front. Some had a large porch and gardens in the back. At night, the warm glow of gaslight fixtures, which hung on the interior walls, softly illuminated the lace-dressed windows.

Annie was one of three children. Her parents put her in the bedroom that had a window facing Anne's (an arrangement the girls had begged for in the weeks before the move), while her older brothers shared a room on the back side of the house. With their windows facing one another, the girls' creative minds used the space between them in clever ways that enchanted their childhood.

As Anne now sat at the table finishing her breakfast, she thought of the sign language the two girls had invented in the first years they lived next door to each other. They'd exchange extravagant gestures from window to window, acting out their messages to one another.

Anne remembered drawing hearts and fish and birds in the winter frost on each of the panes, or a message in letters scratched in the ice. She could still hear in her mind the sound of their voices whispering to one another through the warm heavy air of dark summer nights as the scent of lilac blossoms rose from shrubs below.

One year, with the help of Annie's brothers, the girls put up a connecting rope with pulleys. They passed notes to one another and shared hair combs and dolls, delivering them in sacks tied to the rope.

The girls learned of Morse code in the spring of fifth grade. The following summer they practiced and perfected it together while sitting on the cool floor of the public library. They used it throughout their adolescence, tapping on their window sills messages too private for anyone else to hear or to find written in a note.

When the girls were twelve, it was in Morse code that they had admitted to each other their notice of the Murphy brothers. Fortunately, they each preferred a different brother. Anne liked the older brother, Tom, while Annie liked the younger brother, Charlie.

The day of the blue dress and the church picnic was the first time the boys had paid attention to the girls.

When the brothers were together, Charlie was a whirlwind of action and humor, while Tom was a quiet though amused sidekick.

Through their teen years, the two couples had a wide circle of friends with whom they socialized – most often for dances or card games. But often it was just the four of them spending an afternoon together, canoeing on the Merrimack or picking berries in the meadows beyond the city.

Anne was drawn to Tom's reserved manner as well as his reliability and confidence. Tom had black hair, crystal blue eyes and fair skin. He was already nearly six feet tall when Anne and he met.

Annie's lively personality was a match to Charlie's outgoing nature. Charlie was shorter and heftier than his brother, his eyes were brown and his hair red. In the summer, his skin freckled.

By the time the girls were twenty,
and the boys were twenty and twenty-one,
each couple was married.

"Mama?" Maggie's voice brought
Anne out of her daydream of the past.
"We'll need to leave in 20 minutes. Let me
clear your dishes. Do you want to sit in
the parlor till we go?"

"Alright."

With Maggie's help, Anne moved to
the parlor, though she had not yet
returned fully from her thoughts of Annie.
Once she was sitting comfortably in her
chair, she allowed herself to see and to feel
the rest of the story.

The new young wives settled into
their roles of making homes. They each
gave birth to boys during the second year
of their marriages. With no thought of
tragedy before them, the young mothers
awaited the arrival of their second
children during the fifth year of their
marriages.

Anne's delivery came in the spring.
The birth of her daughter went smoothly.
But during the summer, Annie's delivery
of her daughter went unexpectedly awry.
The baby girl survived but hours after the
birth, Annie died.

Anne became enveloped in profound
sorrow. For months, she hardly spoke as
she nursed the two newborns and began
to raise Annie's children alongside her

own as Charlie declined into despair. Once he returned to work, he would spend the evening with his brother's family and his own children. But he was as quiet as Anne. And he drank. Many nights he'd sleep in the chair where he'd poured his last drink. Some nights he'd stagger to his home and its devastating loneliness.

Anne's daughter was named Elizabeth Anne and soon became known to all as "Lizzy." Annie's baby was christened Katherine Anne, and she was called by her full name all her life.

The girls' earliest months of life were a blur to Anne. While her parents and Annie's parents cared for the boys, Thomas and Charles, who were named for their fathers, she and the nanny spent night and day caring for the infant girls. Anne, worrying that her sadness was a threat to it, willed her milk to not dry up.

As Anne now sat lost in these thoughts, tears dropped to her lap, just as they had fallen on Katherine Anne all those years ago. In those days, when her tears fell, she'd pray to Annie to bless them, and in her mind, with Annie's intercession, her tears during that time were as holy as the water in the fonts at the church.

The months turned to years, and Charlie lost his job when his drinking began to interfere with his work. He sold his house and moved in with Anne and Tom. When he could find no steady work, he did odd jobs to help the neighbors and he maintained Tom and Anne's house while Tom worked in the advertising office of The Lawrence Evening Tribune, the city's most popular newspaper. Out of work and with no routine, Charlie drank more and more. Before he turned thirty-five, Charlie died of a broken heart, and a body broken by alcohol. Anne and Tom were left with the full responsibility of the children.

Anne found it difficult to accept the loss of Annie and Charlie. She never spoke of their deaths, though she always spoke of them, especially Annie, as if they lived on alongside her own life. The children grew up with Annie's presence as sure as every living person around them. Annie was like a guardian angel to them all. If one of the children had a nightmare, Anne would soothe them.

"Don't be afraid, Annie is watching over you. No harm can come."

All the children knew who their birth parents were, but each called Anne and Tom "Mama" and "Pa." Yet it was as natural as can be to hear Anne say to young Charlie or Katherine Anne, "Your Mama is so proud of you," or "Your Mama is full of love for you," or "Your Papa's strong arms are giving you a big hug."

They knew she was referring to their parents in heaven.

Tom never spoke of his brother or Annie. Each morning he'd get up and by rote he'd make his way, day by day, through those early years. He was as reliable as a clock. And when he came home from his workday, he greeted the children with equal affection and love.

Still, there were times when Anne would come into their bedroom at the end of the day to find Tom wiping tears from his face. His heart had been shattered by the loss of his brother and the friendship the couples had shared. Those nights, in silence, Anne would hold him and comfort him. But it was six years before their family grew, with the arrival of Jack. Three years later, Maggie was born.

Through the years, Anne never heard one expression of doubt or a complaint from Tom though she knew that, especially during the Depression years, he lived in fear every day. It was not just the number of children relying on him. It was an awareness that two special souls lived in their midst, the two children who carried the spirit of his brother and his brother's wife, who was Anne's best friend. That was the only difference the parents felt about the children – and it made them feel that they could not fail Charlie and Annie.

Throughout their marriage, Anne and Tom had come to view one another as the half that completed a whole. They each knew that neither could manage caring for the children alone. When Anne saw Tom come up the front walk after his workday, she drank in the sight of him as if satisfying a thirst she'd held through the day. They would greet with a hug and would feel their bodies melt into each other, relieved that they were near each other again.

"We need to leave now, Mama."

When Anne opened her eyes, Maggie was kneeling by her side, holding her hand. Anne was still lost between the past and the present, between memory and reality. So the purpose of Maggie's interruption was not clear to her. But she always trusted Maggie. She stood up from her chair and, taking her daughter's arm, Anne walked out the door in her blue dress to wherever Maggie was leading her.

II

Mid-Morning

Anne reviewed each house and building they passed as Maggie and she drove to the funeral parlor. Anne had lived all ninety-five of her years in this city and knew every street and structure. The city had gone through several periods of change in her time. Though many of the houses were now sided in vinyl, some retained the original flourish of detail that characterized the era in which they had been built. Some Victorian homes were painted in colors that reflected their original palette – multi-colored and bright.

When they stopped at a red light, Anne looked across the wide lawn of the city's common. In her memory she saw children climbing the trees as red, white and blue streamers and American flags fluttered in a breeze while people assembled as close as they could to the bandstand. A smile came to Anne's face and she asked Maggie, "Do you remember when Dorothy Lamour came here?"

Maggie had blended memories of playing with friends during various celebrations on the common. She was ten years old when Dorothy Lamour came to Lawrence.

"I remember that she came here selling war bonds, but I don't remember her exactly."

Anne continued in her quiet, tremulous voice.

"It was 1943 and we were all excited that a Hollywood star was coming to our city. The common was decorated with red, white, and blue everywhere."

She smiled and turned toward Maggie.

"They made the grandstand larger to accommodate all the city officials," and here Anne laughed, adding, "...every man from one side of the city to the other tried to find his way to a seat near her!"

Anne paused briefly, remembering.

"Well, as it turned out, she sat beside the mayor's wife and spent most of her time talking with her."

She turned again toward the common as her mind gazed into the memory of the brightly decorated green that was crowded with people.

"Everyone was playing a part. We were proud to. We were proud of our city's contribution. Our factories made the fabric for the boys' uniforms; some of us grew Victory gardens. Do you remember ours?"

Not really expecting a reply, Anne continued.

"Some women worked in the hospitals – after some training. They were needed. The hospitals didn't have enough nurses. They'd gone to the war."

She paused.

"Our war wasn't like any of yours. We were all in it together. No one ever said, 'What are we doing?' Our sons were fighting. Boys from the neighborhoods were off to the European front or to the Pacific Ocean. Imagine, boys who'd never before been farther than Lake Winnipesaukee."

Silence hung between them. Maggie saw her mother's eyes turn away from the window and gaze toward her hands, which were resting in her lap. With her right hand, Anne fingered her engagement ring and wedding band, an absentminded gesture familiar to Maggie.

Maggie thought of the little cache of memories she had of the boy who grew up twelve years ahead of her in their family, one of the boys sacrificed in that war.

"Annie will forgive you," Maggie whispered, knowing the question that always visited her mother's mind when she thought of young Charlie.

"He was such a good boy," was all her mother could ever manage to say.

Some minutes passed and, looking out the window once more, Anne recalled the families who had occupied the homes she watched flash by. She knew the events that had brought joy and sorrow to the households. When she saw the rusted chain-link fence bordering an empty lot with tufts of grass growing through cracked pavement, she thought of the corner market that had stood in that place when she was a young girl. She'd walked to it often, buying meat pies to bring home for a Saturday night supper.

The stream of images and fragments of stories passing through her mind were interrupted by Maggie.

"Mama, the plan for the day is that we'll be at the funeral home for an hour for any callers, then Father Casey will lead us in prayer. Then the casket will be closed."

Maggie paused to give her mother time to understand the meaning of the moments she'd described. She saw her mother give a slight nod and turn toward her.

"There's no one left to come, Maggie. All our friends are gone now."

Maggie let the comment go. Yes, all of Tom and Anne's friends were gone, but with their large family and many family friends the funeral home and church would be crowded.

Although Anne had helped with the planning of this day, Maggie knew she didn't retain the details, and so she continued to guide Anne in the schedule for the day.

"You can decide if you want to stay in the room when the casket is closed. Just let me know. Alright?"

"Yes."

"Then we'll get into the limousines and go to the church. It won't be a High Mass, Mama. We're doing just what Pa asked, a simple funeral Mass."

"Yes, I know."

Each of the women was now quiet, unable to speak, their sadness at the loss of husband and father halting their thoughts and stifling their voices.

In a bit, Maggie continued.

"After the Mass we'll go to the cemetery. It will be a short walk for you from the car to the graveside. Chairs will be set out so you can sit during the service there."

Anne heard Maggie but made no reply.

Maggie continued, "Then we'll be going to Eric's."

Here, Anne turned to Maggie and smiled a hesitant smile that her daughter had come to understand as an expression of sweet, questioning confusion. Maggie had gone a thought too far or to a detail not immediately familiar, and her mother needed more explanation.

Never wanting to make her mother feel self-conscious about her bewilderment, Maggie spoke more slowly, and expanded and rephrased the last bits of information.

"When Father Casey finishes the prayers at the graveside, we'll get back into the limousines and go back to the funeral parlor. Then we'll get into our own cars and drive to Eric's. You know, Eric is Tom's youngest," she trailed off, giving her mother time to put the meaning in order.

Maggie continued, "It'll be a bit chaotic with everyone there, especially the children. We'll have something to eat and then I'll take you home and get you settled in. Mama, remember - I'll be staying with you till you're ready to come and live with me."

Anne smiled. "I love to be with the little ones."

Maggie knew her mother's thoughts had stopped at the mention of the children. Though she no longer could keep track of whose children they were, Anne's greatest joy came from being near the youngest of her offspring.

Anne said, "All day, I'll just follow you." She smiled at Maggie, who smiled too and reached across the car seat to hold her mother's hand.

Maggie was quiet as they drove the final blocks. Caring for her mother was a distraction from her own sadness about her father's death. At the same time, caring for her mother had a sorrow all its own. Maggie found herself thinking of fireflies – those miraculous bugs that fill a summer night, randomly illuminating bits of space with a brilliance that thrills any who see them. She found herself wondering what happened to the bugs. Did they fade out? Or did they die in an instant, taking their full light in that final moment? She decided that her mother was like a fading firefly, her illumination dimming with the passing of each year and each month, and, recently, faintly flickering off and on as if approaching the end. With this thought, Maggie's sorrow doubled as if in this day she were losing both parents.

Maggie slowed the car as she approached the parking lot to the funeral home. She could see her young grandchildren, three of the boys, running through the lot, heedless of their surroundings – not aware yet of the decorum of mourning, nor conscious of the danger of playing in a parking lot.

Anne watched them with simple pleasure.

"Oh, look at the boys running!"

Once the car was parked and the women had gotten out, the three boys ran to their grandmother, simultaneously giving her hugs. Then, one by one, they turned to their great-grandmother and showed the instinct, the awareness, young children have to be gentle with the elderly. Their faces red from their game of chase, their little-boy ties askew, they stood perfectly still just a few feet from Anne, each taking a turn saying softly, "Hi, Nana," and the two older boys following up with, "Sorry about Pa," as Maggie had instructed them to do.

With her trembling hand, Anne stroked their cheeks while smiling at them. As each boy felt the softness of her touch, he received the grace imparted by the family elder. Though they would hardly remember her one day, they would never forget the tenderness of her hand on their faces and the quiet, halting words that let them feel the love she had for them.

"Are you boys having fun?"

"Yes," they answered together.

"You are fast runners."

The two older boys said, "Thanks," as the youngest smiled in reply.

Then the youngest, wanting so much to share with her, said tentatively, "I cut my finger today."

Anne's natural mothering rose up.

"Oh, show me."

He held up his small hand, dirty from play, so she could see the new cut on his finger.

"Does it hurt?" Anne asked.

"Not now, but I cried."

His eyes nervously looked toward his two cousins as he suddenly became conscious that this admission diminished his standing with them. But they did not dare tease him in front of her.

Knowing these things, Anne said to him, "Well, you are a brave boy."

While Anne could not distinguish one boy from another, nor could she properly attach them to their families, her maternal love came through to each of them. Maggie, witnessing the illumination, felt assured and comforted by her mother's living presence.

Following Maggie's instruction, the boys hurried into the funeral parlor as Anne took Maggie's arm and they walked in behind them. A hush went through the room as Anne's family turned to her. Each responded with a helping hand, or a hug, or tears brought on by a swelling in the heart, which left them unable to step forward at all.

No one could tell which of them their beloved nana remembered with certainty, though that was less important to them than her loving greeting which gave each the sense of being her favorite, so fixed was her gaze when she spoke and so genuinely warm her touch. Seeing her feebleness, everyone was aware of how special it was that she was still with them. In this setting, on this day, they all wondered when they would return here to honor her passing.

Every eye was upon Anne as Maggie led her to the open casket. Anne stood at the kneeler. She felt an uncertainty.

"Is that him?"

"Yes," Maggie reassured her.

Anne looked intently at the face of the body in the casket.

"Well, I suppose it is, but it doesn't really look like him."

"Remember, he lost a lot of weight in the end, Mama."

"I suppose."

Anne put her hands on the rail of the kneeler and slowly lowered herself to her knees to pray for the soul of her husband.

She studied his hands, one placed over the other in a way they never were in his lifetime. She looked at the familiar shirt and tie and jacket, oddly fitting his reclining body. His hair was combed in an unfamiliar way, slicked unnaturally. And the tone of his skin was not right.

But she understood that she was kneeling beside the body of her husband and that he was far, far away – in the past, in her memory, in heaven, she thought.

She reached and laid her hand over his. Immediately she was conscious of the waxy feeling of his skin and the beads of the rosary in his hands. No, these were not her Tom's hands. Silently she prayed, "Eternal rest grant unto him, O Lord, and let perpetual light shine upon him. May he rest in peace, Amen." She blessed herself in the name of the Father, the Son, and the Holy Ghost. Then she asked Maggie to help her stand.

Anne's legs were tired from the effort of kneeling. She shuffled to her place at the start of the receiving line as she held firmly to Maggie.

"Mama, sit as much as you like during this hour."

"I think I'll sit now."

The strain of the physical exertion was evident in her voice. Sitting back against the comfort of a wingback chair she rested. She watched her children, and their children, and the newest generation of her family intermingle and, in hushed voices, share stories and expressions of love that included some gentle laughter amid an overall mood of sorrow.

After a while, the voices became indistinct and the sound of the room a hum that lulled Anne into a quiet state where her mind wandered in dreams.

Anne saw herself holding Tom's hand as they posed for a wedding portrait. She was conscious of the moistness of their palms as each shied away from the extraordinary attention they were receiving this day and as each was distracted by thoughts of the hours and days ahead of them. Needing the reassurance of Tom's promises of love, she pressed the back of his hand to her wedding dress and against her thigh. Despite her nervousness over starting her life as his wife, she was eager to move past the ceremonies of the day.

Her mind's eye drifted, and she saw Tom tenderly holding their first baby, young Thomas. Cradled in his two hands, the baby rested securely as Tom studied his every feature and whispered soothing lullabies.

She remembered the raw blisters on both of Tom's hands, and her own hands carefully applying a healing salve. He had taken his week-long vacation that year to clear scrub and to plant the new plants that would make up the yard of their new home.

Thinking of her husband's hands, Anne stirred in the chair as a familiar phrase turned in her thoughts, "Remember, Man, that thou art dust and unto dust thou shalt return." She became aware of her surroundings as Maggie leaned over and said, "Mama, Father Casey is here."

Anne's faraway gaze slowly focused on the priest who knelt on one knee beside her.

"Hello, Anne. You know how sorry I am for your loss, but you can be certain that Tom is as close to God as any of us can ever hope to be."

"Thank you, Father."

The priest held her hand an instant and then stood to offer his condolences to the other family members. Next he walked and knelt before the casket, grieving himself for a man whose death touched him personally. This was the priest's second assignment to this parish, his first five-year stay occurring when he was a young man, not long out of the seminary. Tom was then middle-aged, and the young priest had come to admire his quiet strength, his unassuming demeanor, and his tireless work for his family and his church community. The priest knew that

Tom was as generous as his circumstances allowed when the basket was passed at Sunday Mass. But more impressive to Father Casey was Tom's discreet hiring of a carpenter or plumber or electrician for any repair needed in the church or rectory or the elementary school that his children had attended. Often, Tom paid the bill himself.

In recent years, during his second stay in the city, Father Casey had visited Tom regularly, bringing Communion to him when Tom was too sick to attend Mass. On those occasions, after the formalities of the Communion were finished, the two men would talk about the Red Sox, and they would support one another's dreams of glory for the season and declarations of disdain for the Yankees. Always, when Father Casey left their home, he would find himself thinking that this aged couple's simple and genuine goodness was not often seen. While the parishioners looked to him for counsel, he looked to Tom and Anne.

He cleared his throat as he stood and turned away from the casket. The gathered mourners could see the sorrow in his face as he announced that he would lead them in prayer. Opening a small book he'd taken from his pocket, he began.

"A reading from the prophet Isaiah – 'But now, thus says the Lord who created you; fear not, for I have redeemed you; I have called you by your name and you are mine. When you pass through the water, I will be with you; in the river you shall not drown. When you walk through fire, you shall not be burned; the flames shall not consume you. For I am the Lord your God, your Savior.' This is the Word of the Lord."

Following the priest's prompt, there came a murmured response of "Thanks be to God."

Then the priest continued, "The joys of happier days can never be taken from us. Let those joys soften the pain of our suffering now. Lord, help us accept this time of sadness. We ask this through Christ our Lord."

Closing the book, the priest continued, "Tom and Anne have been a wonderful example of Christ's intention that we love one another, that we accept all joys and burdens as part of God's plan. Today, let each of us remember the ways in which Tom showed Christian goodness to us and let each of us share his example throughout our own lives."

After leading the recitation of a decade of the rosary, the priest went to Anne and expressed his sorrow again. He reminded her that he would be saying the funeral Mass and that he would be presiding over the burial. He also promised to visit her at her home within the week.

Anne thanked him. She sat quietly, her mind hearing bits of the prayers just said and her thoughts adrift in scenes that included Tom in both the here and the hereafter.

Her thoughts were interrupted by Maggie.

"Mama, the casket will be closed now. Do you want to stay in the room? Do you want to see Pa once more?"

"I'll just sit here."

From her vantage point Anne could see the casket and the imitation silk of the cushioned interior of the open half of the lid. She could not see Tom and she had no desire to look again at what appeared to be a facsimile of him. As she watched her children say their last goodbyes to their father, as they shed the tears of the mortal, her heart ached. And when at last the casket was closed, her heart broke. In that act, she felt the finality of being separated from him and their life on Earth, forever.

Maggie returned to Anne. Seeing the tears that filled her mother's eyes, she wondered how this frail being could tolerate this day. A deep silence filled the room until the funeral director began to usher the family to the waiting cars. Maggie helped Anne stand and walk out of

the room. Without looking toward it, Anne
walked by the casket.

III

Late Morning

Riding in a limousine, with her family all around her talking quietly of the day, of their father, of their children, Anne knew she'd be cared for. And as can easily happen on such occasions, an attempt at humor caused a unanimous cringe. Jack said to his brother, "Hey, Tom, looks like you're 'old Tom' now!"

Anne was so used to the sound of their banter, even at their advanced ages, that the comment passed by her. Aware of the insensitivity of Jack's comment, her son Tom reached to her and held her hand. She smiled at him, and looking into his eyes she saw the little boy he'd been and in her mind she saw the young mother she'd been. She turned and looked out the car's window but saw only the baby in her arms. She stroked his soft face as he held on to her finger and contentedly nursed. She looked up from his face and laughed as she saw Annie sitting across from her, nursing her own newborn son. The new mothers sat in young Tom's nursery, each in a rocker, and as they nursed their newborns, they talked about the tiniest bits of change they saw in their infants' growth and behavior, about their husbands, about their pure joy at having babies to raise together.

Out loud in the car, Anne whispered with happiness, "Can you believe it, Annie?"

Hearing her, Anne's children stopped their talking and glanced toward their white-haired mother who, while gazing out the window, showed peaceful delight on her face. They knew she was visiting a place held in the mists of her mind, a place that was a refuge from the reality of this day.

The limousine came to a stop in front of St. Mary's Church. This mammoth Gothic structure was the setting of one hundred years of history in Anne's family. Her parents had been married there in 1890, when the church was not quite twenty years old. She and Tom, likewise, had married there, as had Annie and

Charlie. All their children had been baptized over the same baptismal font, and young Charlie had been buried after a funeral Mass at St. Mary's in the early spring of 1943. Though her children moved out of the city after they married, the girls' weddings had taken place at St. Mary's. For any bride, it was an intimidating, long walk down the aisle of the church. In fact, for that reason, Anne had chosen to have a small wedding ceremony in the shrine, which was connected to the side of the church that ran along Haverhill Street just blocks from Anne's childhood home. While the church had an awe-inspiring grandness, in the intimacy of the shrine a visitor felt close to holiness itself.

When they entered the church, Maggie helped her mother to the ladies room and she marveled as she watched Anne stand before the mirror and touch her hair to be sure it was presentable before she joined the congregation.

As they walked slowly down the long aisle, Anne held Maggie's arm. It was a slow, tedious effort for Anne. When they finally reached the front of the church, Maggie helped Anne into the pew. While Maggie knelt and prayed for a moment, her mother sat resting, and she settled into what was as comfortable a place to her as her own home. She blessed herself

– touching her right fingertips to her forehead, then to her chest, then to her left shoulder, and then her right shoulder, finally clasping her hands together in her lap. This motion came as naturally to her as smiling, waving or walking. This ritual of blessing herself lifted the barrier between her earthly life and her contemplation of God - a state of mind from which Anne received grace and inspiration, as she set before her Maker her gratitude for blessings and her supplications for help while she silently repeated the "Hail Mary." This was her way of praying.

Anne's eyes looked toward the main altar and to the side altars, and noticed those things - candlesticks, flower vases, statues - that were as well-known to her as the things in her home on her bureau or her countertop or a table in her parlor. She assessed the altar linens with a critical eye. As a young woman she had cared for the linen runners that were prepared for the chalice and crucibles and the gold plate that the priest's host would rest in before the Consecration. That the linens be pressed to perfection was still a standard she held. She was satisfied with their condition this day.

Through the subdued notes of the organ, Anne heard the steps of people filling the church, the thud of dropping kneelers, and the creaking sounds as they were knelt upon. She heard the whispering of adults and the not-yet perfected whisper – quiet talk, heavy with forced breath - of the young children.

Anne's senses were filled with familiar sights and sounds and scents - flowers and burning candles and the lingering, faint aroma of incense - that were a comfort to her.

From the back of the church to the front, a hush came in a wave as the priest met the arrival of the casket just inside the church doors. Family members watched and listened as he sprinkled the casket with holy water while reciting the prayers that remind the living that by their baptism, when they first entered the doors of the church, they began their life in Christ - and that with their death, their life reached perfection as it joined with Christ. Then Tom's coffin was draped with the white pall, which was reminiscent of the baptismal robe.

Led by the young altar server holding the vigil candle high and the priest holding the Bible, a slow and somber procession of pall bearers – Tom's sons, Tom Jr. and Jack, and four of their sons - protectively and carefully guided the casket down the center aisle.

Anne was startled when the organ came to full life. Maggie leaned toward her.

"Pa's being brought in now."

Understanding Maggie's cue, Anne stood with effort as the congregation rose. Everyone faced the altar, but nearly to a person, each glanced sideways as the casket passed by. Some stood still and composed, others wiped a tear from their cheek, and one young woman far along in pregnancy – Anne and Tom's great-granddaughter, Katie - sobbed quietly, her shoulders moving up and down with each quick and sorrow-filled breath. Those around her wondered, did she cry from memories of Tom? Did she cry for her baby who would never know him? Or did she cry for Anne, who was this day losing her one, true, lifelong love?

The casket was set before the altar, just a few feet from Anne. She looked at it and then looked away. Her eyes followed Father Casey's steps as he walked behind the altar and raised his arms to begin the opening prayers for the Mass as the organ music quieted.

Anne looked at the casket again and remembered the first time she attended a funeral. This memory returned with every funeral she attended and today was no different. When she was young, in a church packed with heartbreak, a fifteen-year-old classmate was being laid to rest. The families of the city were in shock in the aftermath of the collapse of a wooden runway that dropped scores of young boys into the swift current of the Merrimack River.

Sitting in the pew now, Anne recalled her vantage point in the church that day, which showed her the look of anguish on the faces of Joseph's parents. He and nine other boys of the city had drowned in the river on the previous Saturday afternoon. With summer just underway that day in June, the sun's heat had brought many boys from the city to the opening day of the municipal bathhouse. While they were waiting for the doors to be unlocked, the weight of the boys on the crowded runway leading to the bathhouse had caused it to collapse beneath them. Despite the great efforts by people who rushed to the scene and who saved many lives, ten families lost a son.

Anne could still see the image her mind invented the day of Joseph's funeral. Dressed as she saw him each day in school, she imagined him being greeted by vague figures of her making, who she thought to be his ancestors in heaven.

For days after the tragedy children all over the city had recurring nightmares, and they sought comfort by climbing into their parents' beds. Anne remembered that her parents were awake each night as she came through their door. It seemed as if the whole city could not sleep – that, in the darkness of the night, the residents felt the terror of the underwater world where the boys lost consciousness and life.

The bathhouse tragedy came soon after the strike of 1912, an event that put Lawrence in the world news. Cities everywhere watched to see how the labor strike would impact conditions for all mill workers. Remembering the reports of violence and the police forces that came to Lawrence to establish order, Anne recalled this as a time when it seemed as if her world were reeling out of control. During these events in her adolescence, she was not young enough to be shielded from them, nor old enough to put them in perspective. She remembered them as being unsettling.

Now, as tears fell from Anne's eyes, her family, sitting in the pews around her, was sure she was present in the sorrow of her husband's death. But Anne's sadness came from a memory that was eighty years in the past, when she was in the snug embrace of her mother as her father stroked her hair and brushed tears from her cheeks

Anne's gaze turned to the altar where the priest completed his welcome to the congregation. As he began the opening prayers of the Mass for the Dead, Anne felt

Maggie's hand take hold of hers and give it a comforting squeeze.

Anne's life had become tethered to Maggie's. Through the years, each of her children had helped her and their father in some way. Jack took care of house repairs, Tom managed their finances, and Katherine Anne did weekly food shopping and other errands. Each Friday, Lizzy came and made a big dinner for her parents, allowing plenty of leftovers to help them through the week. And always she arrived with a freshly made cake or pie. In the evening, Lizzy would read to her parents from a book, or help with a puzzle, or orchestrate a game of Scrabble. She knew it was important to keep their minds active, to keep them alert and current. She'd stay the night, and in the morning she'd do a few chores before returning home.

But Maggie took personal care of her mother. She accompanied her to doctor appointments, helped her bathe, brought her to hair appointments, and gave her soothing back rubs with scented lotions. Though Maggie's love for her mother was no greater than that of her brothers and sisters, she had a greater ability to express it - and Anne felt that love.

Anne knew she was being pulled toward the afterlife. While her body was in the physical world, her mind wandered about in the past, was aware of the present, and was moving toward a real though not fully revealed future.

Anne was comforted by knowing that, while those she loved had died, the love between her and each of them still existed and would be enjoyed again in that future place. She knew that when she died, she would rejoin the completeness of love, and she'd be in a realm of joy. This idea of afterlife brought her a sense of peace.

But she was not yet there. So she lived in a mix of three realms - her mind's wanderings in memory, the current tangible world, the vague glimpses into afterlife - and not totally in any one of them. Her tangible world was becoming the least sure place. But always, if she drifted too far from it, Maggie was there to bring her back to what was - for now - still real. And Maggie herself had an uncanny way of knowing when her mother needed her touch.

They both knew a day was coming when Anne would drift beyond Maggie's reach. As they looked into each others' eyes at this moment in the church, each was keenly aware of this.

Their attention returned to their surroundings, and they both turned toward the altar when they heard, "A reading from the book of the prophet Isaiah." Anne's grandson, Jack, was reading from the Old Testament. Comforting phrases settled on Anne - "... on this mountain the Lord of hosts will provide for all peoples...he will destroy the veil that veils all peoples...The Lord God will wipe away the tears from all faces." He finished the reading and said, "The Word of the Lord." The congregation quietly replied, "Thanks be to God."

As Jack returned to his pew, Anne watched her son Tom approach the altar, genuflect, and then settle himself at the lectern. He reviewed a page from the New Testament and then he began, "A reading from the letter of Paul to the Romans." Again, phrases that soothed those in mourning reached the congregation - "... the sufferings of this present time are as nothing compared with the glory to be revealed for us."

Following Tom, Lizzy read several passages from Psalm 23. Anne heard the voices of her family respond with the consoling phrase, "The Lord is my shepherd, I shall not want."

Father Casey stood at the lectern next and said, "A reading from the Gospel of Luke."

All rose to their feet, and with their right thumb they made a small cross on their foreheads, then on their lips, and then over their hearts. The Gospel reading juxtaposed the key elements of their faith – God's intimate and unwavering love for each of His children, "...even the hairs of your head have all been counted, so fear not..." and the frightening uncertainty of when the Second Coming and individual judgment will occur, "...be prepared for an hour you do not expect..."

When it was time for Communion, Father Casey stepped down from the altar and came directly to Anne. He held the host before her and said, "The Body of Christ." She replied, "Amen" – and in that one word was the crux of Anne's faith, "I believe." Knowing that the custom of her generation had not left her, without hesitation the priest placed the host on her tongue.

Anne knelt and said a prayer of thanksgiving after receiving Holy Communion. She thanked God for her health and her long life and her happiness with Tom. She thought of Tom's final days of suffering and she asked God to cradle him in a painless, peaceful state. She found relief in knowing her prayer would be heard and that Tom could now rest.

She sat back in the pew, quietly contemplating each person approaching the altar to receive the host. She did not see anyone receive on the tongue as she had. She did not see anyone approach

Communion with palms together in front their chest, and head bowed, as she'd been taught as a child and as she'd done her whole life. She watched her family members put out their hands with varying degrees of reverence, and then put the host into their mouths. She thought how different were the rituals of the current day. In her day, a person would not dare touch the host. Her generation had been instructed that the consecrated host was too holy to be handled by anyone other than a priest.

Though they were odd to her and seemed not right, she didn't question the new ways. She let them be, trusting that over time all these things would be sorted out in accordance with God's plan.

Anne saw young and old pass by her as they turned away from the altar and walked back to their seats. She found herself studying the face and stature of each person. She pondered, as she often had through the years, that this collection of her descendants, this assembly of family, which now belonged to her alone, had started with a mix of first cousins who had been raised as siblings.

She could no longer separate the family-tree branches that delineated Tom's and her children from Annie's and Charlie's. It was a mix of people that shared Tom's and Charlie's genes, and that clung to her as the queen bee. She cared for them all with thoughts of Annie always in her mind.

As Anne thought about Annie, she became overwhelmed with the sense that Annie was there with her in this moment. She could feel her, as a physical being, right there beside her. She closed her eyes and held Annie's hand. And when she did, she had all the assurance she needed from Annie that she had done a fine job. Anne was weary, and this confirmation from Annie made her cry.

Maggie, still kneeling after her own Communion, turned when she heard her mother quietly sobbing. But seeing her mother's eyes closed, she decided to leave her to her thoughts. Slowly, Maggie sat back in the pew, but she did not reach to Anne or whisper a word.

There was silence in the church as the priest cleaned the chalice and went through the ritual of removing from the altar all that had been used for the Consecration and Communion. When he sat for his own moment of meditation, those who had been kneeling sat back also, and the creaking of the kneelers and the benches momentarily broke the stillness.

After a minute of complete quiet, Father Casey rose from his chair. The congregation then rose, too. He raised his right hand, and drawing the sign of the cross in the air, he bestowed the final blessing. And when he said, "The Mass is ended, go in peace," the congregation responded solemnly, "Thanks be to God."

Anne returned abruptly to the present when she heard these closing words. She was startled and sad when she realized Annie was no longer with her, and she was relieved when she turned and saw Maggie sitting beside her.

IV

Noon

Somber organ notes filled the cool air in the dimly lit church as the family followed the casket down the center aisle. The sound tugged on strands of Anne's memories, teasing from them a scene from her childhood.

As she walked alongside Maggie holding her arm, in her mind's eye Anne saw bright sunlit images from her childhood days when her family spent summer vacations at Lake Sunapee in New Hampshire. Early Sunday morning they would ferry to Great Island where a congregation gathered under a canopy, and a small, portable Estey organ would fill the air with floating notes that had no walls to deflect them or to absorb them. In

her child's mind, the notes were like
butterflies riding the air. The farther they
moved from their source, they mixed and
mingled, then blending with the sounds of
their setting – the rustle of a breeze
through the trees, the songs of the birds,
the quiet lap of the lake's water on the
muddy shore.

Holding securely to Maggie's arm,
Anne walked out of the church and into
the sunlight. She thought of her mother,
whose hand she'd grip in shyness when,
after Mass, the vacationing families would
stand in the morning sun and share
gossip about the prior week's activities
around the lake.

Anne was brought out of her dreamy
thoughts when Maggie said, "Be carful
here on the steps, Mama," and then
walked with her to the waiting limousine,
where Maggie helped Anne settle into her
seat.

Anne watched and listened as her
family entered the car. After the Mass, a
solemn mood came with them, and when
their silence settled around her, her eyes
became alert to the details of the
dashboard. Everything was black or silver.
She saw knobs and buttons, dials and
lights - but her tired mind did not care
about any of it. For many years now, the
technology of the world had advanced as
her use of things had diminished. All that

remained for Anne were basic functions - eating with a fork, sitting in a chair, sleeping in a bed. Few objects still linked her to the concrete world. The dashboard before her held no meaning and stimulated no thought. As her eyes looked at the controls of the car, her mind thought only of Tom. When the car began to move, she felt that she was being drawn closer to the end of the day that would take Tom from her forever.

The procession of cars moved slowly through the streets of the city. In time, the hillside of the cemetery came into view. Stone markers of various sizes were scattered about an expansive green lawn set against a silvery, pale blue sky. The cars drove between the stone pillars at the cemetery entrance and wound along narrow lanes. Each person in Anne's car saw the markers of graves bearing the names of families they knew well.

The hearse had led the way and it now stopped at a freshly opened plot. Anne's car pulled to a stop just behind the hearse and she sat still as Tom's casket was taken carefully from the hearse and carried to the prepared site.

In her ninety-five years, Anne had often witnessed this scene. This day the sight did not have any greater meaning to her than at any other time. Stark life was laid before her in a visual scene so that she, and all others who were there, saw what life held in store for each of them.

When the casket was in place, Anne was helped from the car. Jack and Tom stood on each side of their mother and took baby steps as she held their arms and slowly made her way across the uneven grass to the graveside. They helped her sit on a white metal chair - the legs of which sank slightly into the newly thawed surface of the ground when she sat down. Father Casey was already positioned at the head of the casket. Anne sat just behind him, to his right.

As her family quietly assembled around the casket, no one was fooled by the carefully placed tarps, which were there to cover the mound of soil. And though sprays of flowers were set down in a way to keep from view the cement slabs that lined the hole in the ground, they were visible enough for each person to see and to contemplate.

Jack unceremoniously turned to Tom and said a little too loudly, "Please don't let them do this to me, brother. Burn me and scatter me in the woods." Tom smiled at Jack reassuringly.

Anne could smell the fresh soil and, as Father Casey began the graveside prayers, the scent of the earth brought her memories of kneeling beside small garden plots in the backyard of her home.

Decades before this funeral scene, when the four oldest children were very young, Anne had opened the earth one spring day, cutting out four small flower beds. She had guided the children in poking the cool soil with their little fingertips and instructed them in the way to properly space the inch-deep holes.

She had them reach into paper envelopes and take out seeds. She showed them the wondrous differences between the various flower seeds, knowing she was giving a much broader life lesson as she spoke. Their small hands, not yet skilled for detailed work, often dropped too many seeds into each indentation. She showed them how to refill the holes with soil and to gently pat each finished planting. Though she knew mud would come into the house afterward, the lesson continued with watering each of the flowerbeds. And for the next few weeks as the children ran about the yard, the sun's warmth and spring showers worked their miracle, and shouts of joy filled the air when green shoots broke through the soil.

Years later, when Jack and Maggie were young, Anne helped them through the same lesson. And still, as adults, all of them would look into her yard when they visited - fondly remembering the excitement of tending the gardens year after year.

Anne now sat in the sun
remembering that as her children moved
from home, she looked after the
abandoned beds. In the quiet years of her
life, without young children to care for,
she found gardening to be a meditative
exercise. And her thoughts often turned to
the child whose garden she knelt before.
She'd think about her children's individual
natures and how those traits had
remained with them into adulthood. It was
no surprise to Anne that it was Maggie,
always the empathetic soul - the most
constant caretaker of her garden bed, the
nurse to wounded birds, and the dear
heart who visited elderly neighbors – yes,
Maggie was naturally the one to attend to
her personal needs in her declining years.

Far back in her mind, Anne could
hear Father Casey speaking, but her
daydream overrode the moments she was
living through, and Anne's thoughts
continued. She remembered how she
could easily spend hours each day
throughout the springtime savoring the
smells of the earth and the fragrances of
her perennial plants as she gardened.
Each year her lavender shrubs barely
survived the winter, their green color
turning a dull gray on many branches.
But still, the plants would let her know
they had life as they released their dense

scent into the air when she brushed against them as she worked.

She'd run the palm of her hand over her varieties of thyme, and lifting her hand to her face she'd smell their intense aromas - lemon thyme was her favorite. She'd pinch a sprig of marjoram between her thumb and forefinger and, smelling her fingers, she'd think of recipes for its use.

When her annual herbs came up, a new array of scents filled her garden that later rose from summer dishes whenever her family gathered for a cookout. Her basil barely grew fast enough to kept up with the requests that she serve sliced tomato, hand rolled mozzarella and basil leaves, drizzled with olive oil and balsamic vinegar, all topped with a dusting of black pepper.

A breeze gently touched Anne's cheek and brought her attention back to the cemetery and where she sat. Father Casey was sprinkling the casket with holy water. Anne saw the sparkling droplets on the casket's polished wood and she thought of morning dew.

V

Early Afternoon

The limousine pulled into the funeral home parking lot. Anne was helped from the car. Maggie stood with her and spoke to her about the next phase of the day. She told Anne that they would now drive to Eric's house, a twenty-minute ride to the countryside in the neighboring town of North Andover. Anne just smiled and patted Maggie's arm. With this gesture, Maggie knew that her mother really had no idea what she had said. It was barely noon and Anne's capacity to hold on to the realities of the day were already diminishing. Maggie didn't bother to explain again. With a rush of sadness, she knew that Anne would follow her over a cliff, she was so trusting of Maggie's lead. Maggie kissed her mother's forehead. "Come on. Here we go."

As they walked to the car, Maggie could see in her mother's slow step that the morning had tired her. The spring sun had warmed Maggie's car despite a chill in the April air. So, she was not surprised when, within the first mile of driving, Anne fell fast asleep. Seeing her napping, and hearing the slow deep breathing of sleep, Maggie thought of her own children – who, as toddlers, would fall fast asleep once in the car after a morning at the playground. Thoughts of life's cycles passed through Maggie's mind.

As Maggie wondered of what her mother was dreaming, Anne was enjoying a dream in which she was gliding through the early summer waters at Lake Sunapee, her winter-weary muscles matching her desire for strenuous exercise as the water caressed her dry and thirsty skin. The warmth of the sun on her back kept the chill of the water tolerable until her body generated its own heat. With each powerful stroke and each intake of air into her lungs, she heard the muffled sounds of her body's work - the rush of the water around her as she kicked and glided, the alternating quieting of sound as she'd turn one ear to the water with each stroke of her crawl, and the exhale of air from her lungs.

She was a young mother and it was with tremendous freedom that she enjoyed her swim, knowing Tom's watchful eye was on the children. She was shedding a year of mothering as she swam, and her body relaxed as it became her only concern. No child was calling to her; no sticky little hands were holding on to her skirt.

Here she was in the waters of her childhood. She was welcomed by the water. Her parents swam in these waters and now, too, did her own children. And as she thought these thoughts her exercise tipped into that sensation of having no body at all. All things were in concert: her breathing, her stroke, her strength, her drive, her self. She was fully alive. It was in this state, the sensation of feeling free of her body, that she felt closest to God.

Maggie turned into the driveway of her nephew's house and parked the car in the space left for her, nearest to the front door. She had extended the ride to let her mother have a good nap.

Anne stirred as Maggie turned off the car. She looked about until her eyes saw Maggie. Anne was self-conscious and amused by her own confusion.

"Where are we?"

"At Eric's."

Maggie hoped this information was enough to orient her mother. But Anne continued to gaze about with no apparent recognition.

Maggie thought quickly.

"Father Casey spoke such nice words after the prayers at the gravesite. He genuinely liked Pa. And I'm glad he remembered to mention this gathering at Eric house."

Anne turned to Maggie who looked pale and weary.

"Oh, right."

Maggie was glad when her brothers came out of the house and helped her walk their mother inside.

Anne sat in the living room, feeling a bit refreshed because of her nap. She was the subject in the lens of each person's line of vision, but each had the reserve to not overwhelm her with attention, except for one little boy who walked right up to her.

"Hi, Nana."

"Hello, Angel." Anne used her pet name for each of the children.

"Pa's getting buried now."

"Yes, he is."

The boy's mother spoke above the chatter of the gathering.

"Tommy!"

The boy glanced nervously toward his mother and then redirected his conversation.

"Your eyes are really, really blue, Nana. I like them."

"Thank you."

"My eyes are hazel. That's what my mother says. It's like green but not exactly."

"Yes, I see that. Pa had hazel eyes."

"He did?" The boy was puffed-up with pride.

"You look like Pa."

Tommy settled into a chair next to Anne.

"When he was a boy, you mean?"

"Well, yes, when he was young."

"Did he get in trouble at school?"

"I suppose sometimes he did."

"I do, a lot. My teacher says she doesn't know what to do with me."

"What should she do with you?"

As if the answer were absurdly clear, Tommy raised his voice slightly and said, "Just let me do my work if I'm sitting or I'm standing or if I'm humming!"

"That sounds reasonable."

The boy spoke in sing-song imitation of his teacher.

"She says, 'But what if everyone was standing and humming?'"

Returning to his natural voice he said, "I tell her, 'No one else is, so who cares?'"

Anne gave a startled look.

"And what does she say?"

As he answered, his whole body wriggling in further mocking.

"She goes, 'I do!' - I don't say it, but I think in my head, 'So what, if you care!' "

"Well, it's good you don't say that. She might think you were being fresh."

"I'm not fresh."

Barely pausing, Tommy continued.

"Nana, have you seen a killer whale? Do you know how big they are? I went on a field trip to the aquarium. They are called a killer whale so I thought it would be...like filling this house. But it's not. It's smaller. Like filling this room and that room," he said pointing to the dining room.

"Really?"

"Really. I want to do scuba diving so I can go near one in a cage."

"Where is one in a cage?"

Anne was fully absorbed in the conversation.

"No. *I'd* be in a cage in the water with a scuba tank on. That way it can't eat me. They said that it won't eat people, but I want to be in the cage to be sure. Sometimes they do that with sharks – the scuba diver's in a cage."

"I think that sounds safe."

"My mother doesn't think so."

"Well, maybe when you are a little older."

Tommy's eyes scanned the room and a table with trays of food on it caught his attention.

"Do you want a cookie?"

Anne smiled and knowing she'd please him she said, "I'd love two."

"Yes, m'am!"

Tommy then leaned in close to her face, so close that she could feel his breath as he whispered, "Don't let Kevin sit here when I'm gone. Okay?"

"Okay!"

Anne smiled at the sight of his shirt tails hanging over the back of his pants as he hurried away, and she thought that he's the little one who is always so nice to her, though she didn't remember who he was among all the children.

Because of his name, she wondered if he were Tom's grandson.

The boy's mother took his absence as an opportunity to speak with Anne.

"Is he bothering you?"

"Not at all. He has the most wonderful thoughts to share with me."

When Tommy returned, he said, "I got me three and you two. One of mine has chocolate all over it. You can have some."

His mother stood to give him his seat.

"Be polite to Nana," she warned as she left them to continue their conversation.

Anne took the cookies he held out to her, and as he bit into one of his he asked, "Nana, did Pa cry about dying?"

"No."

"Was he scared?"

"No, I don't think he was. I think he was ready."

"I'll never be ready. I want to live to be..." and pausing, the boy considered a minute and then continued, "...well, infinity."

Anne saw, by his direct look into her eyes, that this was a question. So, his Nana smiled at him and said, "I think that's a good plan," leaving open the chance that this was a possibility.

"I'm going outside now."

Tommy abruptly stood and dodged and bumped his way through his family. Anne knew he'd be back and she looked forward to his return.

Tommy's mother came back to Anne and sat where he'd been.

"Thanks for being so kind to him, Nana. He loves you. He tells me all the time how much he loves you."

"Well, I love him. I don't mind at all talking with him; he's interesting, like a little scientist."

Her words landed on the mother's hopeful heart that everyone would be so open to her bright boy.

As the afternoon continued, Anne's family members came and went from her side. When she appeared to tire, they let her be and she drifted off to sleep. Just before she slipped into a dream, her mind realized of whom Tommy reminded her - he was like Charlie Jr., who was always a good boy in her eyes, though others seemed to be less patient or to misunderstand him.

As she slept, she dreamed about young Charlie. She saw him running up the front walk, a school paper in hand.

He was calling, "I got an A! I got an A! My first A!"

Anne beamed with happiness for him. She dropped to one knee as he came bounding through the door, so that he could run into her open arms. He hugged her with all his might.

"I did it! Mama, you said I could and I did. And it wasn't hard at all. I love spelling!"

He showed her the test and said that his teacher had held it up in front of the class and said a rhyme.

"Mark the day, Charlie got an A!"

He said everyone had clapped and he had bowed three times.

The dream ended with his twenty-two-year-old face smiling before her. As always happened in this dream, just as she'd relax in the comfort of seeing him, he'd grimace, his eyes would close, and he'd drop to the muddy ground in a smoke-filled field as deafening explosions would awakened Anne.

Anne startled. Her eyes filled with tears. Stirred from the world of dreams, she was aware that people were around her in a room. But she cast her gaze out a nearby window and thought of the boy running up the walk to her arms. She longed for the time she would see him again. She remembered her last moments with him, her heart unbearably heavy as she drew a cross with her thumb on his forehead and sealed it there with a kiss. Though he was hurrying to board the train that would take him on the first leg of his journey overseas, he was patient with her in the moment. In his youthful exuberance, he could not imagine that this was the last time he would feel her loving touch.

In the final, fleeting seconds of his life, as he closed his eyes to the world, he saw her face and felt her kiss upon his forehead.

Maggie came to Anne with a tissue and knelt beside her.

"Are you thinking of Pa?"

"No."

"Charlie, then," Maggie said with certainty. "Well, Pa's with him now."

Anne looked into her daughter's eyes and spoke with exactness through her weary voice.

"Maggie, don't cry when I'm gone. It will be the happiest day for me – to be with your father and to hold Charlie again, and to see Annie. Don't shed one tear."

"I'll do my best, Mama."

With the back of her fingers, Maggie caressed her mother's face and then kissed her cheek. Anne's tired eyes expressed her love for Maggie.

Anne's great-granddaughter, Katie, walked over to Anne and Maggie.

"Hi, Nana."

"Katie, Nana's been remembering Uncle Charlie. Here, you sit with her a while and cheer her up with stories from your classroom! I need to help Katherine Anne in the kitchen."

Katie was glad to sit beside Anne. She took her hand.

"You okay, Nana?"

Anne tried to smile.

Katie knew Anne was still too upset to speak. So she did.

"I've been so sad today. I can't stop crying. I think I made a spectacle of myself in the church. I'm especially sad for you today. You were with Pa for so long. I'm so sorry, Nana." With a worn tissue Katie dabbed her eyes.

Anne knew Katie well. She often visited Anne and Tom at their home. Anne and Katie were kindred spirits. Anne tried to console her.

"I know, Sweetheart. Pa and I were together for a long, long time. We were blessed to have each other for so long."

To help her grandmother find some relief, Katie asked with as much lightheartedness as she could muster, "So, have you been writing any poetry lately?"

This question was a secret code between them. They each loved poetry and each had tried her hand at it.

Anne smiled as she answered.

"Well, not really."

This had been her reply for several years now. But the repetition didn't stop Katie from asking. Always, she hoped that her Nana would write one more. And she didn't want to stop asking and cause Anne to think she didn't consider her still capable of writing.

"Have you been writing, Katie?"

"Well, I've been really busy with work and I've been tired with the pregnancy. But to be honest, expecting a baby has opened a whole new piece of my heart and I am scribbling thoughts on scraps of paper all the time."

"That's wonderful!"

"Sometime, maybe after the baby is born, I'll go through it all and write."

Katie paused and thought a minute.

"Nana, have you thought of your best poem today?"

Anne was so glad to be with someone who was sensitive to her.

"Yes, I've thought of it today and I thought of it often in the last few days."

"I have it with me in my purse, the copy you gave me."

"I'm so glad I gave you a copy of it."

"It means so much to me. I love you, Nana."

Anne gave Katie a gift in return. "I love you, too, Katie. You have my heart."

Anne reached and held Katie's hand.

Katie received her great-grandmother's heart into her own as Anne held her hand and her gaze.

Anne turned away from Katie and for several minutes she looked out the window to the blue sky. Soon she tired and her eyes closed as she drifted off to sleep. Katie cried softly, understanding to where Anne's thoughts had wandered.

VI

Mid-Afternoon

When Anne awoke, her son Tom was sitting at her side.

"You okay, Ma?"

"Yes. Where are we, Tom? Is it far from home?"

"No, not far. You're about twenty minutes from your house. We're at Eric's - you know, 'out country' in North Andover." Tom used a phrase Anne herself used, hoping to orient her.

"Oh, right. Maggie told me that. I just can't seem to remember much lately."

"It's okay, Ma."

Anne's quiet son sat quietly at her side for several minutes. Then he asked, "You hungry?"

"A bit."

Without a word, he got up and went to fix her a plate. When he returned, he arranged a side table for her.

"Is that okay?"

"Yes, Tom, thank you."

Anne slowly took small bites, just enough to nourish her.

As she ate, Tom shared his thoughts in his own halting way.

"Pa had a good long ride."

He paused before adding, "You'll be okay, Ma."

Anne had loved her son Tom longer than any of her other children, simply because he was the first born. But she also loved him in a way that was different than the rest. As a little baby, he had adored her. As her only child for three years, she could dote on him. And his love brought out her best love.

Their time alone ended abruptly, the spring the girls were born and Annie had died. Never again did they share time as they had before the girls came. And even today, thinking about it, Anne could feel the grief she often felt when she'd look upon her young family at the dinner table and she'd catch Tom in the corner of her eye – his devoted gaze locked upon her, more as an instinct than actual memory. Always, when she saw this look in his eyes, she'd go to him and give him a hug and a tender kiss, hoping that her expression of love would fill the void she knew he felt, though he didn't understand why.

Sitting there now, Anne reached and took his hand.

"I love you, Tom."

"I know, Ma."

But he could never really know, because he could not remember, as she did.

After a while, guests began to leave and only family members remained in the house. The afternoon was passing, though the sun had not yet begun to set.

Jack came into the room and, much louder than necessary, said to his mother, "Ma, are you remembering my birthday's next week?"

Anne's tiredness could be heard in her answer.

"Oh, that's right, it is."

A bit louder, Jack asked, "Will you be making me a cake?"

Tom closed his eyes, let his head rest on the back of his chair, and smiling in amusement he muttered, "He's setting you up, Ma."

Not catching on, Anne answered, "We'll see."

"'We'll see?'" Jack bellowed as the house went quiet, and a call came from Katherine Anne in the kitchen, "Oh, Jack, not today!"

Ignoring her, with a big smile on his face, he yelled for all the house to hear, "But Ma, I'm your baby!"

Hearing his words, there was a stampede of feet running throughout the house and calls of, "Uncle Jack's gonna say it! Hurry up! Hurry up!"

And the children, their faces beaming with expectation, came from all corners.

Even the teenagers ambled into the room with amusement on their faces, while wishing they were young enough still to participate in this part of their Uncle Jack's ruse.

The children danced and hopped around him crying out, "Maggie's the baby! Maggie's the baby!" while the older boys called out, "Say it! Say it!" and the older girls called out, "You better not say it!"

Jack let the frenzy reach its peak and then, with great drama, he roared, "Maggie's not the baby! She doesn't count! SHE'S A GIRL!"

With that line delivered, a family tradition was under way. The children let out a deafening cry.

Pleased with the results of his performance, and with much fanfare, Jack led the children out into the sunlight. He broke the spell of what had been a somber day, and for the next two hours they laughed and played as children should. With just a bat and a ball, he organized the family's favorite ritual, a batting contest – the girls against the boys. Through the years the family kept a record of the contest's dead-even results.

While Jack kept the children busy at play in the yard, their fathers helped him coach the game as their mothers began the clean-up inside the house. Periodically, the women would take a break from their work to watch out a window as their child or grandchild was at bat, or to comment, "Their clothes will be ruined," as they saw those not at bat tumble and wrestle in the soggy grass of early spring. Even Tom had followed the rush out the door, and this shy man watched his brother's animated personality in wonder and amazement.

Soon after Jack's dramatics, Maggie sat by her mother.

"He got you again, didn't he?"

Anne laughed. "He does every time."

Maggie smiled. Though she was the brunt of Jack's joke, she loved the immediate and long-term outcome of his mischief with the children.

Now that she was sitting, Maggie realized just how tired she was and she didn't hurry back to the kitchen. As her body relaxed into the chair, she made small talk with her mother.

"Lizzy's fixing us a supper for later, in case we get hungry."

"That will be nice."

"And I'll be staying with you, remember."

"That will be nice, too."

After a few minutes, Maggie made a subtle mental shift – the shift that realigns people with the reality of the greater world, after they've stepped out of it when personal tragedy strikes.

"Gosh, the children might all have homework they need to get done for tomorrow. Jack had better bring them in soon so they can get home."

Maggie got up and went outside to begin redirecting the children. But Anne's mind didn't move forward with Maggie's. She found herself deep in thought about Tom. She thought of his absolute true love for her. Sometimes, when he looked at her with his pale blue eyes, she became so caught in the love of his gaze that it was as if she and Tom left their bodies behind them, like discarded skins, and they met in a place between, a place where their spirits joined.

When he held her in his arms and ran his fingers through her hair they would each relax into an existence that was not physical. Anne could never think of a way to define this suspended state. She had come to think of it as true love, or pure love, or real love. When they were together, the perfect form - the essence of love - came to be. They were no longer physical beings but love itself.

There was no one Anne could talk to about these things. Never did she hear another woman talk of her marriage love in any way that would entice her to try to speak of her love with Tom. But once, in a poem, she tried to express her understanding of it.

As she sat quietly, Anne assembled the lines of the poem. She had written it during the time that Tom and Charlie were in high school and she was influenced by their studies, especially their science study, which was fascinating to her. So, she wove that into her words. Now, bit by bit, the whole poem came to her.

Our Love

Characters in order,
arranged into a thought,
can't say what's between us
when near you I am caught.

Is it biology or physics,
or a combination of the two,
in that place between us
when I stand by you?

No molecules, no structure,
nothing we can touch,
in that space between us
where I love so much.

What is it that lingers
and hovers there unseen,
in that realm between us -
it's more than just a dream.

It's warm, it's dense and heady,
we sway in its spell,
while there it lives between us,
no bottom in its well.

Is it a bit of you, or a bit of me,
or a blend that's we?
In that place between us
where I join you, and I'm free.

Anne turned and looked to the sky,
her old eyes seeing sparkling floaters in a
sea of blue. With all her heart she
thought, "I love you." And then she closed
her eyes and slept again.

An hour later when she awakened,
she spent a minute getting her bearings.
The voices of the children at play still
carried through the air as the sun sat low
in the sky and lengthened the shadows in
the last light of the afternoon.

Anne was alone in the living room
and she felt detached – as if she were no

longer part of the energy of the living. For her to share in the real world, it had to come to her. For her, simply walking now required that someone be by her side. She thought that if no one came for her, this is where she'd die. While the same sense of dependency would cause an infant to wail for attention, at this end of her life the thought did not upset her. In some ways she felt as if she were already gone, as if she were slipping into being a memory, a sideline spirit alongside her family. It was as if, when they saw her, it was already a nostalgic event.

Through a doorway to the kitchen, a motion caught Anne's eye. She saw Katherine Anne crouch down and tend to a toddler. Katherine Anne was still stunningly beautiful at age seventy. Her once auburn hair was now luminous white. She wore it as she always had, just more than shoulder length and held in a large barrette at the back of her neck. She still was tall and fit. As Anne watched her kiss the child's cheek and smile her love upon the child, she felt great relief. Here was the evidence that Anne saw, only in recent years, that Katherine Anne was at last at peace.

Of all the children, Katherine Anne was the most accomplished. She'd attended Wellesley College – not because she was the smartest of the children, but because she was the hardest working. Yet this was the child Anne had worried about most. Her achievements came at a cost – she had not found balance through her youthful years. She had been intense and sometimes emotionally distant.

When she was very little, Katherine Anne had asked Anne on occasion, "Did my mother die because of me being born?" Anne assured her: "No. God wanted your mother in heaven. He needed her there." Desperately wanting an answer, the little girl would ask, "Why?" And Anne would say, with real faith, "For reasons we don't know. Only He knows." This didn't seem to satisfy the child, and she'd go quiet for days.

For Anne, it was a bittersweet blessing that Katherine Anne had Annie's beautiful eyes and long black lashes. When Katherine Anne was young, Anne could almost feel Annie's presence when she'd look into the child's eyes. But although the physical form was there, the joy in living was not, as it had been in Annie's. So, Anne would see a dull representation of Annie's lively eyes, and this would cause Anne anguish and concern that she wasn't doing enough to make this child happy.

Through the years, Anne watched Katherine Anne go about life with a drive that she knew could not be healthy.

Though Katherine Anne was always good, Anne wished she'd learn to be a little less good. She filled her days with schoolwork and chores and giving attention, much more than was necessary, to her brothers and sisters. She'd organize performances, and design backyard games, and in later years she'd drive them where they needed to go, advise them about their schooling, plan family celebrations of birthdays and holidays. While it was a great help to Anne, she would try to stay a step ahead of Katherine Anne in an effort to keep the hierarchy of responsibility in place, and to dispel from Katherine Anne the sense that only she herself had, a sense of obligation to make up for what she felt she'd taken from them all – Annie's life.

For years Anne worried that this drive had cost Katherine Anne her happiness. She'd married a nice fellow. But he also, Anne thought, was stilted in his emotions. Their days seemed to be defined by things that needed to be done. For them, there was no ease of living that Anne could see, despite their accumulation of wealth. And through the years, Anne had been concerned for their children. They were expected to achieve. And while Katherine Anne and her husband seemed to be this way by nature, their children were not. So, there was much unnecessary pressure on the children.

At some point - maybe it was when her children became self-sufficient, or perhaps when the grandchildren were born – Katherine Anne had mellowed, as if a great exhaling had occurred and she let go of her self-imposed burden. Whatever the moment, whatever the cause, Anne was relieved to see Annie's daughter finally relax - and to begin to give and to receive love, and to be content and happy.

Turning away from her view of the kitchen, Anne suddenly felt a rush of exhaustion. She wondered where Maggie was. She wanted to go home now.

At that moment, Tommy arrived - a whoosh of movement through the door and right on up to Anne's face.

"You're awake!" he said with an exuberance that seemed to inform as much as to observe. He had passed by the doorway several times while Anne slept and he had waited till he saw her stirring to visit with her again.

"Yes, I am. And I'd like you to do me a favor."

Taking a step back, Tommy stood still with self-importance, ready for his instructions.

"Sure, Nana. What do you want me to do?"

"Could you please find your Aunt Maggie and tell her I'd like to go home now."

Tommy looked into Anne's eyes. He saw something there. But he was too young to know what it might be. He only knew she needed his help. He replied to her slowly and with calm sensitivity, though for what reason he was not sure.

"Okay. I'll hurry, Nana."

"Thanks, sweetheart. You're an angel."

"*You're* an angel."

Tommy turned and hurried off to find his great-aunt.

Anne straightened the skirt of her dress and ran her trembling fingers along the edges of the collar and cuffs as she waited. She felt funny, not sick exactly, just uneasy. She reviewed what she'd eaten and wondered if something had upset her stomach.

It seemed to take an eternity for Maggie to finally arrive.

"Hi, Mama. I was outside looking at Katie's new van. She's just bought it - getting ready for family life!"

Then Maggie saw that her mother seemed unsettled.

"Do you feel alright?"

"Yes, I guess I do. I'm just awfully tired."

"Okay, I'll tell the boys and we'll walk you to the car. But let's get you to the bathroom first."

Maggie helped her mother out of her chair, and across the room, and through the kitchen, and into the bathroom. Maggie heard the shuffle of her mother's steps and the exertion in her mother's breathing, and she intently watched each step for any sign that her mother might fall. Maggie felt her mother's energy fading and she consciously shared her own as she helped Anne with a most fundamental human need.

Jack and Tom helped Anne to the car. Maggie saw their tenderness toward their mother. While they were giving her direct personal attention, at the same time there was a formality to their actions, and a respectful discretion in their demeanor. They loved their mother in a way that was singularly for her, and perhaps there is no love in humanity as innocent and untainted as that of a son for his mother. But still, they held back. They spoke softly to her, in broken phrases, and brief sentences. "Okay, Ma," "You're okay now," "Here now, watch it here," "You're all set," "We got ya." Their eyes looked at her with helpless sorrow. In that look, Maggie saw what they all knew - despite their ages, when their mother died, at her wake each would stand like an orphan, bereft and lost.

The children gathered around the car as Maggie started the engine. She put down the windows so they could say goodbye to Anne. Some just called, "Bye, Nana." Others came to the window and gave her a kiss. Tommy kissed her and said, "I hope I see you soon, Nana." Anne smiled. "I hope so, too."

Lizzy called from the front door of the house, "I'll stop by with a supper for you!"

Maggie waved in thanks to Lizzy.

VII

Late Afternoon

On their way to Lawrence, Maggie drove over country roads, through North Andover's old center with its brick general store and its bygone hay scales building, past the lovely common with its beautiful variety of old trees that shaded much of the lawn, and on down Massachusetts Avenue, and into Lawrence. In the last stretch of mile before the city line, the Ayer Mill Clock Tower filled a portion of the sky. The four-sided brick tower stood high above all other building tops.

Looking at it, Anne felt the sensation its presence always gave her, the feeling of being home. From vantage points throughout Lawrence, the clock tower was a visible point of reference. Like the North Star, it oriented the inhabitants of the city. And it reminded the residents of the remarkable history of Lawrence. It was a source of pride.

Maggie said, "I think this is my favorite view of the clock tower."

Anne smiled. "Every view is my favorite."

And it was true. Seeing the tower had always calmed her. It gave her a sense of place.

But as they drove closer to it, and it filled more of the sky, Anne began to see the night ahead of her. She was returning to her life without Tom. So, as the clock tower welcomed her, there was a new and odd awareness – a question really: where was home now?

"Are you okay, Mama?"

"Yes."

They now were within the city streets and the tower was out of sight.

"I can't really see anything more."

Thinking she meant the tower, Maggie said, "I can drive by it again if you like."

Anne's reply sounded vague.

"No."

Maggie had missed Anne's meaning. Anne's mind was stuck. It couldn't grasp the idea of being at home without Tom. She couldn't imagine what her life would now be – she couldn't see what was to come.

Anne had faced loss before. She knew grief. But this was different. What she was experiencing was an absence for which there was no acceptance. For the first time, Lawrence did not feel like home - because Tom was not there.

Maggie parked in Anne's driveway.

"Well, we're here."

Anne looked out the car window toward the house, but said nothing.

With some effort for both women, Maggie helped Anne out of the car, along the walk and up the three steps to the stoop at the back door. She helped her mother over the threshold and, once inside, helped her change into her housedress. Maggie went to the kitchen to heat water for tea, leaving her mother in the parlor, to her thoughts and to the relief that Maggie hoped the familiarity of her home would bring.

Shortly after, as Anne and Maggie drank their tea, Maggie said, "Katie had your poem to Pa with her today. She showed it to me. I hadn't read it in years. It's such a beautiful expression of love. How did Pa react when you gave it to him? How old were you then?"

Anne spoke haltingly as she answered Maggie.

"Well, I wrote it as a gift for our twentieth anniversary. So, I must have been forty. Your father had a good heart. I know you know that he was a good, good person. But he held a lot in. He didn't talk too much about anything personal – mostly his goodness came through things he did."

Repeating herself, Anne said, "I gave him the poem as an anniversary gift. We didn't have any extra money to buy gifts then. When he saw the poem written on the paper, he asked me to read it to him. So, I did."

Here, Anne paused and smiled as she reflected back on her young self.

"I was self-conscious. I'd worked on it for days and I'd thought it was a good poem. But suddenly, reading it aloud to him, it seemed a jumble of words. It had become so familiar to me I couldn't hear it as he was. But when I looked up from the paper – and I'm sure I was flushed with embarrassment – your father had tears in his eyes."

Anne sat quietly, her own tears coming to her eyes as she relived the moment.

"The poem has stayed in his bedside table drawer since that night."

Maggie sat still, thinking of the love she'd seen between her parents, a love she'd never found. Of course, in the thrill of falling in love with her husband, she'd thought she'd found a love as true as her parents'. But soon she'd learned it wasn't.

In fact, she'd likened her relationship with her husband to the description of a style of play that is witnessed in children – parallel play – when two children play alongside each other, glad to be in close proximity as each is busy with an individual activity.

In recent years, when Maggie was with her women friends and they'd talk about what they'd termed "the states of their unions," Maggie would find that her repeated reply was, "We're still in our simpatico holding-pattern," knowing this was a more amiable connection than the descriptions from her friends of their marriages.

Maggie was drawn out of her thoughts when she heard her mother ask, "Will someone be coming for that?" Maggie followed her mother's gaze. Anne was referring to the hospital bed that for the past two weeks they'd all come to see as a necessary intrusion in the parlor.

"I think they said they'd come for it tomorrow, Mama."

Though he spent his daytime hours in the hospital bed, Tom had slept beside Anne all but his last few nights, when he no longer could be moved comfortably. But for portions of those nights, when she was not sitting by his side, Anne would retire to her bed, and with the bedroom door left open, she could see him, and those who tended to him, through the doorway.

Thoughts of the coming night were too much for her - so she shut her tired eyes and dozed her way into a deep sleep.

VIII

Evening

When Anne awoke, the parlor was in darkness. She heard voices coming from the kitchen. Through a window, she could see the trees silhouetted against the remaining light of the fading, dark blue sky.

She called out, "Tom?"

From the kitchen there was a reply.

"No, Mama, it's me, Maggie. And Lizzy's here. Let me put on a light for you."

When the light came on, Anne felt even more confused by her surroundings.

"Why am I sleeping here? Is Tom home yet?"

Maggie and Lizzy exchanged glances and then both came and sat on the couch on either side of their mother.

Lizzy spoke.

"Mama, you've had a long and tiring day. You just fell asleep here in the parlor."

She eased into helping her mother recapture the day. "I'm glad Maggie got you home and settled. And I've brought some of the leftovers from Eric's. If you're feeling hungry, I'll fix a plate for you."

Anne looked at Lizzy. She thought about eating. She was hungry.

"I guess I'll have a little something. Could I have some water, please?"

"Yes. Of course you can. You can have whatever you like, Mama!"

Lizzy would have given her the world in this moment. For in her mother's eyes she saw that Anne was letting go, that she was detaching from those she had loved her whole life. She could see that Anne didn't know her. Anne didn't recognize that she was talking to her own daughter.

Maggie saw the same thing. She hoped her own voice would help orient her mother.

"While Lizzy fixes us something to eat, I'll walk with you to the kitchen."

Together, her daughters let out a sigh of relief when Anne replied, "Thank you, Maggie. You've been such a help to me today."

Both women wondered if it had been their imaginations, Anne's momentary disconnection. But each knew that their instinct was right, Anne was slipping from them. Maggie hoped it was just the strain of the day and that, after a few days' rest, her mother would be more alert.

Soon, the moment was forgotten and their conversation continued.

Maggie asked Lizzy, "Will Monica be watching for you to come in tonight?"

"Yes, she always does."

Maggie and Lizzie were reassured when Anne joined in.

"Good. It was so nice of her to be at the funeral today."

What Maggie next said was meant for Lizzy more than Anne.

"Of course she would be there, Mama. After all these years, Monica is a part of our family."

"You're right, Maggie." Anne meant what she said as she thought about how Lizzy and Monica had been friends for years – perhaps thirty years now.

Anne couldn't remember how they'd met. But at some point they bought a duplex together and for more than twenty years they'd lived side by side. And they vacationed together. Since Lizzy had never married, Anne was glad for her companionship with Monica and grateful for Monica's attentiveness to Lizzy's well-being. Monica was a blessing. Just as Anne and Tom had begun to wonder if Lizzy would ever find the right fellow,

Monica had come into her life. Bit by bit, Anne and Tom had stopped expecting or hoping for the right man to come along. Lizzy seemed content. In fact, she seemed happy. And she and Monica were caring and loving aunts to Anne's grandchildren, who had come to refer to Monica as "Aunt Monica".

As Anne sat with Lizzy, she thought about Lizzy's kind and generous heart. She remembered the thoughts she had during Lizzy's childhood, a childhood that caused her to be like a twin sister to her cousin. Lizzy shared her mother's breast milk, her bedroom, her toys, her classmates, her whole life with a sister who was in her life by sad circumstances. Anne's petite, curly-haired, redhead daughter was as unlike Katherine Anne as any could be. Still, the girls loved each other dearly.

Though Katherine Anne was the more grounded and mature, Lizzy was her fierce defender if ever the chips were down. It was Lizzy who'd given a black eye to a boy in fifth grade, when he taunted Katherine Anne about her "skinny, giraffe legs."

When they said goodbye after supper, Anne said to Lizzy, "Please give my love to Monica when you get home."

"I will. Thanks. I love you, Mama, and so does Monica."

When Lizzy had gone, Maggie helped Anne get ready for bed and she found relief in joking with her mother.

"A woman like you needs a lady-in-waiting! We've dressed you three times today!"

Anne smiled and said, "I'm so grateful to you for today, Maggie. Thank you."

Maggie kissed her mother's forehead.

"It's my pleasure, Madam."

Anne chuckled, amused by Maggie's silliness, which was brought on by complete exhaustion.

When she finally had her mother tucked into bed, Maggie stood at the foot of the bed and thought about the start to their day, which now seemed so long ago.

Maggie lingered, and after a moment, words struggled from her heart and through a tightness in her throat.

"Mama, I love you. I admire you. And I am so grateful to you for... everything."

After a pause and after she'd composed herself, Maggie smiled and whispered a chant that she and her siblings had said to their mother on her birthday, or Mother's Day, or any time their affection was focused on Anne.

"Of all the mothers in all the world, we were blessed with the best of the lot."

"I am the one who's been blessed.
Now get to bed. You must be so tired.
Sweet dreams, Maggie. I love you."

IX

Forever After

Maggie closed the door behind her as she left her mother's room. Anne settled under her blankets and saw the last bit of brightness from the hall light dim as Maggie pulled the door shut. Anne was in darkness. Images from the day filled her vision. The past and present played in her mind's eye, on and on and on, until there was nothing more.

She thought of her poem and heard herself reciting it to Tom, long ago.

"To be, for me, is to be with you, at the setting of the sun..."

She brought her arm from under the blankets and reached to Tom's side of the bed. She patted his place on the mattress. "Goodnight, Tom. I love you."

Tears formed in her eyes, and she heard her poem continue, "When darkness descends, as each day ends, with you only, my darling one..."

Anne felt the full emptiness of her life without Tom. Her heart swelled with longing to be near him. She, and her heart, were weary. Sleep pressed heavily upon her. Her eyes closed, and she passed into a welcomed rest.

Tom was with her, as if he were holding her in an embrace, and they were one – just like at the end of his workday, when they were young and they would reunite, and in each other's loving arms they were again whole, they were complete.

"Our love is eternal, Anne."

*****

It was morning and Maggie sat on the edge of the bed. Quietly she cried as she held her mother's lifeless hand. She had found her mother's handwritten poem in her father's bedside drawer.

As she read it and reread it, Maggie understood with profound clarity the nature of her parents' love. It was so real, so alive, that death itself could not rob them of it, nor destroy it.

Nothing had prepared Maggie for this day, for what she was witnessing. She felt as if she were looking through a peephole into all meaning, but was only able to see a tiny though overwhelming piece – that love had power over death.

Through her mother's death - in a simple room, in a simple home, in a worn city - all meaning had burst forth in her mother's last heartbeat. Death could not stop her parents' love. With Anne's passing, death itself had been used by love to keep her parents as one.

What words had Maggie been taught in life, what concepts did she have to draw from now, as she sat here beside her mother? Was it in "and the greatest of these is love?" Should these words have taught her about love's power? She had never considered that these words might suggest that love could overpower death, could use death for its preservation.

While sitting there grieving for both of her parents, Maggie was comforted by knowing that her parents had found the real purpose for living. Through the love they had for each other, they had attained the fullness of life's meaning.

*****

Anne was with young Charlie.
Finally, there was peace in her heart, and

in that peace, pure joy. Never again would she know the pain of losing him.

*****

As much as Maggie wanted this time alone with her mother, she was anxious for any of her family, her brothers and sisters who she'd already called, to please hurry to her.

*****

Reunited in a joy that was beyond earthly understanding, Anne and Annie knew they could not be parted ever - their love would never again be interrupted.

*****

As soon as her brothers and sisters arrived, the getting on with things began. The funeral home was called. Their phones rang non-stop. The visit to the undertaker was scheduled. Throughout the day, the family talked on and on about how remarkable it was that Anne had died so soon after Tom's burial.

And all the while...

*****

...Anne was with Tom and Annie and Charlie and young Charlie. She was with her parents and her grandparents, and with her children and her grandchildren. She was with every generation that

preceded her and that followed her in this earthly life.

Even Maggie, who had tucked Anne into bed the night she died, was already with Anne in this timeless, boundless eternity.

*****

For the remainder of her mortal life, Maggie would not know that her mother enjoyed her presence continuously. On occasion, Maggie would sit quietly, rereading the poem, and she would try to comprehend her parents' love – that neither could be, neither could exist, without the other.

The Setting of the Sun

To be, for me,

is to be with you

at the setting of the sun,

when darkness descends

as each day ends,

with you only, my darling one.

With you I lay –
for this I am –
to be held closely to your chest,
as tender words you whisper
and your hands lovingly caress.

For this I've waited
the whole day long,
to be with you in the night -
hearts together, singing our song,
love birds taking flight.

"Dream of me dreaming of you,"
I whisper as you fall to sleep.
Then in an instant you are gone,

and I softly weep.
For in this moment I know, too,
that a day will sometime come
when your eyes will not re-open
with the rising of the sun.

Then to the blue sky,
and to you beyond,
I will send my plea -
Do not die, or take me with you,
without you, I cannot be.
  -with love, from Anne to Tom

The End